SHE REMAINS

Amika Caruso

SHE
REMAINS

atmosphere press

© 2022 Amika Caruso

Published by Atmosphere Press

Cover art by Jennifer Rose
Cover design by Kevin Stone

No part of this book may be reproduced without permission from the author except in brief quotations and in reviews.

atmospherepress.com

Amika Caruso

SHE REMAINS

atmosphere press

© 2022 Amika Caruso

Published by Atmosphere Press

Cover art by Jennifer Rose
Cover design by Kevin Stone

No part of this book may be reproduced without permission from the author except in brief quotations and in reviews.

atmospherepress.com

CONTENTS

I: Her

Self Portrait - 5
Four Leaf Clover - 6
Orbital Pirouette - 7
Rag Doll - 8
Pearl - 9
Superstitions - 10
Liquid Drops of Gold - 11
Thin Journal Pages - 12
Thinking Too Much About Thinking Too Much - 13
What is a Voice Pt. 1 - 14
She Remains - 15

II: Thoughts

The Past Forgot Us - 17
Stoney Lonesome - 19
Grotto - 20
Better or Worse - 22
Waking up to a Power Outage at 3am - 23
O the Dreams - 24
Butterflies - 25
The Tale of Death - 26
Bing - 27
Snow White - 28
Post Beat Blues - 29
Moments Between Moments - 31
Head in the Sand - 32
Burning too Long - 33
Winter Slugs - 34
Music Goes - 35

III: Love

Liebestraum - 37
Glass Castle - 38
I've Got a Flower in My Palm - 39
I'm in Somebody's Love - 40
Grave Digger - 41
Questions to a Lunar Eclipse - 42
Winter Dream - 43
Wish I Could Write How I Think - 44
Your Voice - 45
Things You Fell in Love With (Not Me) - 46
Cinnamon Skin - 47
Someone is Talking to Me, I am Looking at Them - 48
Arborescent Crows - 50

IV: Remains

On Watching the Sunset - 52
In the Water - 53
Olfactory Hope - 54
Looking So Far Near - 55
Life is Round - 56
A Christmas Carole (Beautiful and Alone) - 57
Looking Asleep - 58
Wired Skies - 59
Untitled - 60
Customer Servitude - 61
Put Me in a Box - 62
Dreams//Memories - 63
Sit - 64
Lotus - 65
What is a Voice Pt. 2 - 66
Notes from a Nap on the Beach - 67
A Poet's End - 68
Old Friends – 69

I:
HER

Self Portrait

A woman enters
    pooling over an empty stage like water
Hair entangling her head with hellish curls
    frizzed and wet with rain
Lips straight like a jacket she refuses to wear
    and refuses to take off
Her nose is sharpened to ward off strangers
    but a soft loam is compressed in her eyes, awaiting
    fresh flowers
Fertilized by worms and a decomposed past
    full of bones and beetles still moving

    Her eyes give her away

She walks with anxious feet, long and slow
    and begins performing a role nobody gave her
Addressing an audience that's never there

    Her eyes give her away

Her bones are charred from summer fires
    leaving her skin a layer of wintery ash
And as autumn brings atmospheric rivers
    water runs and weakens shocked roots
Soil melts into mud and slides down her walls
    crumbling them into small mounds

    Her eyes give her away

Four Leaf Clover

I made dentures out of someone else's teeth
    and no longer recognize my smile

I stole my fingernails from old 4 by 4s left in the rain
    and they are too rusted to paint

I found my hair half-woven on my grandmother's loom
    and she never noticed it was gone

I borrowed an ear from a deaf artist
    and I still hear his thoughts

I found my eyes in a grave
    and they are made of sea glass

My lips were the seal of an envelope
    holding a letter from an old stranger

I broke my arms off the tree my father grew from seed
    right before he cut it down

I put them all together and looked at my reflection in the water
    and the water looked back
    but not me

All these pieces fit like a four leaf clover in a fool's hand
    the lucky leaf severed by his clumsy attempt
    to pull it from the ground

I'm a walking scrap yard of forgotten relics
    and other people's pieces held together
    by sap and glue

But all I can wonder is
    who was looking back from the water
    if not me?

Orbital Pirouette

Careening towards the clumsy cosmos
her ballerina toes leave light
                              trails
                                          of
                                                        l u s t

Catching an orbit on the edge of her twirl
she is pulled to a c o n t r o l l e d glide

Transfigured from dancer to skater
she carves figure 8's on Saturn's rings

Regardless of never tiring of a single solar system
she hardly stays among similar stars long

When comets swarm her
she lets them carry her soft body
                forever
                            farther
                                        a l o n g

Rag Doll

Eating is an activity for the dying
sleeping a sport for the dead

I am filling this body with pins and needles found lying
at the feet of the poorly read

I'll sew together a doll by nightfall
making the final stitches with the fraying strings
that held the clustered stars

She'll sit pretty
dangling cotton legs off a shelf on the wall
while sparrows fly in to press dried cranberries
into her powdery scars

By morning the sky will have fallen
from the seams I tore
and the doll will shred under the cosmic pollen
sprinkling her ashes on some unearthly shore

Pearl

I walked the beach
for years and days,
gathering shells and sea glass
like loose teeth pulled from the mouth of the ocean.

        I mosaicked the pieces into a home,
        carefully placed and heavily grouted,
        polished and glazed to finish.
        I stare at the gum line of old treasures
        and lost ideas.

                My own teeth fell out in a dream
                long before I knew how to remember.
                I've forgotten where I built the door in this place;
                the windows are opaque
                from relentless salt and storms.

        Maybe if I sit here long enough
        the shells will remember their past lives
        and close in on me
        creating a void of pressure,
        compressing me into a pearl.

Superstitions

I keep a safety pin above my left breast
        to ward off danger

And the wing of a Black Witch moth behind my ear
        to attract the dead

I collect chewed pencil ends
        to milk them of their leftover words

And write them on the ashes
        of burnt poets

I eat cloves because I'm afraid of the dentist
        and sleep on a bed of needles to avoid the chiropractor

Morticians purchase the contents of my ash trays
        to fill their urns

Ghosts wear nicotine patches
        when I invite them for dinner

Language is the first lie I told
        and arias the second

The roses I grow in my window wilt before they bloom
        and the thorns keep nail files in their stems

Superstitions keep me alive and close to the end
        like walking a tight rope between real and what else

Truth has always been a lie
        and they say lies are where truth hides

Liquid Drops of Gold

The clouds were liquid drops of gold this morning,
    nobody was around to see them
        save for me.
I soaked them up through my dull eyes
    to steal their glow.

This is where that sparkle comes from
    so many of you have spoken of;
        you thought it was mine,
    I told you it was.

Did I also tell you my favourite quote?
    Burroughs:
Everything belongs to the inspired and dedicated thief.

        Constellations don't have lines drawn between
            them
            yet we see the images somehow,
                when we want.

        There are church windows torn in my tights,
            runs made of stained glass
                and sunlight

        Torn by demons, glazed by Gods
            all through my own hands
                I never recognize.

The stars are liquid drops of gold tonight,
    nobody is around to see them
        save for me.
So I'll cap my broken teeth with them
    and practice a grin.

I repeat my mantra,
    a desperate effort to believe myself:
Everything belongs
    to the inspired

and dedicated   *thief*

I fill my ears incessantly with noise
but it isn't that. It isn't that though
me. There's no way to make sense of it not starting since it's happening and everything that
eyes happening has a beginning and an end. But not this. So there he was. this dark man of
sorts, maybe not even a man, a crow's eye or that would have been weird when man didn't
exist. Maybe he evolved with us. Death, that is. Sometimes I see him in a crow's eyes
though, more often than I'd like in a man's. That's not to say I haven't seen him in a man's eyes
sorrow. So he started out just as we did, as nothing. That's what they say. Then we were
something. Death was the soulmate for Life. They had a beautiful romance in the beginning.
She was so full of everything ever and kept showing him all the magic she could do. He
watched her tricks with amazement and lust and he made them back into dust or sparks
again when she had new ideas. They never got tired of this game. On and on nearly the day
Life making, Death taking, but together nothing was left unfinished or mistaken. I guess it
was the perfect love. But that naive love that you have with your first, where everything is
too perfect and all the giving and taking and making and destroying looks beautiful covered
in glitter but eventually glitter washes away, most of it anyways, in the ocean and in the stomach of a hopeful fish and then in the stomach
Either way the glitter goes somewhere else. I wish it didn't. I'm sure they wish it didn't too.
I think the problem began when Death started looking like a man and Life didn't really look
like anything anymore. It probably wasn't very easy to love nothing. Or for nothing to love
something. Especially something she made. Well, it's easy to love something you make but
it's hard to love it unconditionally. So then, did Life make Death? That line became blurred.
I used to make sense. They made everything, nothing made it all, it all was nothing. Now it
is everything, or something. Who knows? Anyways, the relationship got stale but there's no
way to end it, obviously, but that doesn't mean we haven't tried, and aren't still. Oh man,
some people are trying real hard. What a terrible thing to see, someone fighting with nothing
cause they think it's everything but don't realize they are the same thing. So everyone is
dying just the same but feels like more cause there's more to die and nobody living hardly at
all cause there's too much living and feels like too much dying and we are sick of living to
die and we want to live to live but don't know how when all we are doing is dying. So Life
and Death are sticking it out together, doing a relationship I've never seen, but it's getting
brutal and they are fighting a lot and the amazement is gone from Death's eyes. Ever since he
became a man, a modern man, and Life lost her eyes and she can't see anymore and it's hard
to create beautiful things to look at when you can't see. It really is very sad to stand end now
doesn't it? It's hard to say if it if it ever end though. I personally don't like to think that's
that was so thin is showed the last entries looking like they were all one
ther but so crowded you can't decipher it well it just
erstand what my mind looks like a little bit more now.

Then they are blue
Below the blue sky
Above the blue ocean

Just me
All separate
And yet I know them
All the same

Thinking Too Much About Thinking Too Much

I am trying to understand the different workings of others' minds and all I have to compare and study is my own along with faulty explanations restricted by language and image a mind creates infinite substance unbound-able by the physical and symbolic world how one can think in colours and shapes flashing behind their eyes ideas they cannot immediately convey but must translate them into a form of contemporary culture yet another may assign numbers to their world like a paint-by-numbers kit with a paintbrush moved by experience so there must be endless trains of thought chugging through this far away near dimension and my mind is constricted and restrained to words words words all in English the driest language I ever spoke multiple monologues frog-leaping over each other's backs my skull a lobby full of tourists coming and going forgetting passports and documents never really leaving always coming back not paying for their stay but squatting and pissing on the floors and writing on the walls and getting in fights in the hallways it's a run down hotel that needs a tune up but the super is sick of fixing it up just to see the junkies roll back in and sometimes she even likes the junkies with their character and charisma and dirt under their nails and yellow in their eyes it all looks more real than clean and white after so long of them crawling around the place and some days are peaceful and still it can't always be a mess right so some days the hotel is quiet and the writing on the walls look like landscapes and the piss on the floors look like brambling brooks and everything is okay on those days but eventually the bills go unpaid and the place starts to smell and rot again and it all comes back to the dirt and the yellow and it is okay I guess cause that's normal now isn't it but then someone said that isn't normal for them and the more I talked about it the weirder it was and turns out not everybody's mind looks like that like a lot of people's probably do but not anybody I've really talked to it about with and sure I think that's a good thing cause there seems to be a lot better ways so think like in pictures or ideas or music yeah music would be lovely to think in I hear it sometimes when I really let go in that space between sleep and awake I can hear the music but when I really notice that I'm hearing it it all goes away just like that and the words are back but at least I got to hear it a little and when sleep is good I get to hear it more often but anyways I guess I'm just trying to understand the different workings of others' minds but I don't really understand mine and when I saw this journal page that was so thin it showed the last three entries looking like they were all one page together but so crowded you can't decipher it well it just made me cry cause I think I understand what my mind looks like a little bit more now.

What is a Voice Pt. 1

O how a voice can escape you
in the midst of existing
like a sneeze from a giant
hanging on Jack's bean stock
blowing distant towns into dust
everything crumbles
everything falls

O how that voice plays you
portraying you in sounds
you don't understand
as though its language
isn't the same as yours

O who's voice could this be
coming from this empty mouth
painted on a mannequin
I am told is my body
a story I can't seem to prove wrong

O how a voice can escape you
how it can trap the world around you
this voice is a cloud
surrounding this lifeless body
holding it too far above ground
to feel safe
to let go

She Remains

Standing in an ancient spot
      surrounded by future relics
walls pockmarked with graffiti
      grass groomed with devotion
           to the American lawn
      sprinkled with leaves
           like dust on an old book

                She remains
            still on her podium
                frozen in the dance
                    she had been carved in
            sorrow of the unfinished
                  cracks her chiseled skin
            and she threatens to squeeze tears
                  from stone
            yet she remains

White begins to curve into open air
      emptying space already vast
           creating fogged church windows
    one nostalgic view overlapping another
           the view beyond the glass is unclear
      and she remains
standing in an ancient spot

II: THOUGHTS

The Past Forgot Us

Isn't it all so very staged
these little lives we live
writing pages of past poets' words
and relishing in their meanings
we pour fulfillment into wine glasses
and break off their stems
emptiness persuades us
enticing our clammy hearts to love
jealousy and disgust sweat
in our cracked copper palms

Aren't we all so estranged
in this present that seems already passed
where the flowers grow wilted
and the water has no reflection
we paint ourselves in oils
and sing ourselves in song
but all has been said and done
before us
and time has forgotten to renew

Swinging endlessly on the momentum of man
our hearts flutter over the edge
and stomachs flip above land
but all the while we know we sit secured
on this pendulum swing
hands and chains blurred in the wind
while the sky presses tears from our eyes

Here now lies eternity
written before the romance
of our own hand and pen
fate and destiny mumbled
in mouths muffled by masks
Gods and Goddesses are praised
by faithless priests and pastors
the Hierophant lies hopeless in our hearts
and I dream of lying, resting

in grass grown into the sun

But the moon has ploughed the fields
with his blue teeth
and left all land cold and hard
with naught save for our bodies warm
to light our morning wanders
but bodies grow stiff with time
as does all the world
and quicker now we see
Death walking in our lives

When fear has ruled our visions
love has lost itself blind
and running too long, too far
we wither at our own hand
estranged beings in an estranged home
we built

All days are passed as crosses
and breaths are swallowed as thorns
all days are passed behind us
and the future seems no more

Stoney Lonesome

There are holes in   these boots already
like holes left in the   sky after a moon
less night there's stars stuck to the soles
from all this spacious wandering there's
souls stuck to the   stars from all this
  w o n d r o u s   s p a c e

Their eyes are planets blocking the stars
their eyes are planets brighter than stars
 they talk to me   while I look at them
until the full moon falls beneath my feet
and I kick it   one more rock down the
 streets   to   Stoney   Lonesome

There are still holes   in these boots there
are still holes in the   sky they are still
 talking to me   I am still looking at them
and all I see are the   holes in their eyes

Grotto

I hide away in this grotto

>sitting amongst selves
>pulling things off shelves
>only to replace them
>tinted with a look of grotesque
>hindrance and forgetfulness
>I wouldn't dare leave a thing out of place
>lest a guest come and see the change
>lest they see behind the change

I hide away in this grotto

>observing the body in each seat
>forever staring at their swollen feet
>performing ceremonies to fill glasses
>protecting the clock's blackened hands
>from sunlight and frost
>and I see that I am the smallest hand
>ticking incessantly
>waiting for the batteries to die
>waiting for the seconds to cease

I hide away in this grotto

>counting the ghosts hidden in threads
>and dust bunnies under empty beds
>draped in moth-bitten clothes
>and summoning powerless genies
>by rubbing fools-gold lanterns only to
>burn the papers my wishes are written on
>burn the papers I drew my eyes on

I hide away in this grotto

>alone surrounded by voices
>alone with incomprehensible noises

      alone captured by visitors
      alone inescapable of words
      alone covered in being
      alone naked in nothing

I hide away in this grotto

    alone
    I hide
    alone
    let me
    alone
    let me
    hide
    alone

Better or Worse

Better or worse
    is it
    do you say
    to be a fairy in mist
    than an ant on sand?

Better or worse
    to dye my lenses
    in roadside flowers
    than to polish them clear
    as quartz?

Better or worse
    to bleed all that is left
    into this empty chalice
    for no one to drink
    than to wait for rain
    to fill it instead?

Better or worse
    to make this heart pump
    from shock and fear
    than to let it sit
    still as stone?

Better or worse
    is it
    do you say
    to hurt and live
    than to rest and give?

Waking Up to a Power Outage at 3am

Embers are still maraschino cherries stuck in the digestive tract of my wood stove
    I throw another double on and close the door.
        I burned all my candles to mock the daylight
            so I sit in the moon's dark,
                no choice but to be awake when you aren't
        sleeping.
             I read words I don't know from pages I hate
and rub my eyes when they get stuck between my lashes,
                pressing the legible ones in my journal
                      calling them mine.
            The black of dawn and dusk are twins
                and I think it could still be
                    the night before.
                          No

        It is 3 am
        and the power is out.
I'll have a cup of coffee to prove it
        and raise a cigarette.
                    Two
                          Three
                              Four
                                  Yes.
                        It is 5 am
                    and the power is on
                  and the rain is on
                and the kettle is on
            and the race is on
          and the day is on
      and I am on
    the same page
I started on.

O the Dreams

O the dreams are killing me these nights

> all broken teeth and hives
> all naive love and lies
> all whimsy wishes and cries
> all dirty dishes and sharp knives
> all covered in shit and flies

O the dreams are killing me these days

> all cloudy gloom and no rays
> all nerves set ablaze
> all thought-trains lost in fields of maze
> all feeling drowned in waves
> all bodies hidden in caves

O the dreams are killing me
O the dreams are killing me
O the dreams are killing me

> *Hold on to your dreams*
>   *they say*

O the dreams are killing me
O the dreams will kill me
O the dreams I'm dead

Butterflies

Strangers arrive in your life
like larvae in spring's pond
weird and soft
blurry and easily forgotten

Some may eat their way into your vision
becoming something softer
colourful, a caterpillar of acquaintance
fuzzy images of warmth

Eventually they bloom into beings
butterflies of endless variety
fluttering like eyelashes around your head
and summer is gorgeous
and friends are gracious

Until winter comes and you can't stop it
guilt may drape over you
when the snow and moon
kill them all

The Tale of Death

It's hard to say when any of it really started I personally don't think it did but that's just me there's no way to make sense of it not starting since it's happening and everything that is happening has a beginning and an end but not this so there he was this dark man of sorts maybe not even a man at first because that would have been weird when man didn't exist maybe he evolved with us Death I mean sometimes I see him in a crow's eyes though more often than I do in a man's that's not to say I haven't seen him in a man's eyes too so he started out just as we did as nothing that's what they say then we were something and Death was the soulmate for Life they had a beautiful romance and she was so full of everything and kept showing him all the magic she could do and he watched her tricks with amazement and lust and he made them back into dust for her to try again when she had new ideas they never got tired of this game on and on they'd play Life making Death taking but together nothing was left unfinished or mistaken I guess it was the perfect love but that naive love that you have with your first where everything is too perfect and all the giving and taking and making and destroying looks beautiful covered in glitter but eventually glitter washes away most of it anyways it goes somewhere like in the ocean and in the stomach of some poor fish and then in the stomach of some rich lady but either way the glitter goes somewhere else and I wish it didn't I'm sure they wish it didn't too I think the problem began when Death started looking like a man and Life didn't really look like anything anymore it probably wasn't very easy to love nothing or for nothing to love something especially something she made well it's easy to love something you make but it's hard to love it unconditionally so then did Life make Death that line became blurred it used to make sense they made everything nothing made it all it all was nothing now it is everything or something who knows anyways the relationship got stale but there's no way to end it obviously but that doesn't mean we haven't tried and aren't still oh man some people are trying real hard what a terrible thing to see someone fighting with nothing cause they think it's everything but don't realize they are the same thing so everyone is dying just the same but feels like more cause there's more to die and nobody's living hardly at all cause there's too much living and feels like too much dying and we are sick of living to die and we want to live to live but don't know how when all we are doing is dying so Life and Death are sticking it out together in the longest relationship I've seen but it's getting bad and they are fighting a lot and the amazement is gone from Death's eyes ever since he became a man a modern man and Life lost her eyes and she can't see anymore and it's hard to create beautiful things to look at when you can't see it really seems like a dead end now doesn't it it's hard to say if it'll ever end though I personally don't think it will but that's just me.

Bing.

I just remembered Bing the   old man who wandered the streets of Princeton always   adorned in big wool sweaters and glasses eclipsing   his full m o o n eyes always a l o n e and talking   with someone he gave me hard candies and mom   gave him a hug but eventually he was still a l o n e and talking to no one so t h e y moved him a few towns over and he d i e d eventually I think in his   nineties probably still a l o n e I hope talking with someone   again though but he was really just a s i m p l e t o n man made out of l o v e and really shouldn't   have been a l o n e by then but he was   and that   must   just   be how it is   for   p e o p l e   like   Bing.

Snow White

I left an apple on my nightstand
        and saw Snow White had taken a bite
        while I was away.

Her hair filled the grooves in old records,
her porcelain skin glimmered in thrifted china.
The dwarves had not been back to see
        her poisoned cadaver
and the evil witch was a myth.

I lowered my body beside hers
        and compared reflections in the skylight:
one supple, straight, childlike
        the carving of an ice skate left on
        winter's frozen pond.
The other abundant, curved, womanly
        the ripples on the same pond
        in spring's palms.

Together we lay this way,
        Death and I,
        pondering each other in forms
        I cannot explain

When the dwarves returned, I know not,
        for in her glass hand I saw
        the apple still fresh
And took a shy, sibylline bite
        as had she,
        Snow White.

Post Beat Blues

I crave to find that dark spiraled tunnel
        you see in the Beat's eyes
I beg to find the grave they lay in
        and flip through their rotting dreams
I pray to open one of their heads like a can of soup
        and eat the noodles

An addict is buried beneath all these pages
        in tranced fixation dreaming upon object before him
Just as Jack said to do
        scratching the walls of my words
Counting days in needle straight tallies
        and his face carries many

Hollow, hardly flaked with paper skin
        a skeleton of man satirically stern as the river that
            flows upon hell

A woman sharp and protruding from all the nostalgic places
        a remembrance of a crow through spilled ink and
            feathered fringe

A round and grey fellow with Tibetan singing bowl cheeks
        and hair woven by Judah haphazardly left on the loom

This disembodied head rolls around that box everyone says to
    get out of
        and never can themselves.
Barred by fear
Barred by inauspicious dreams
Barred by batons and articles
Barred by pigs and writers
Barred by media squeezing propaganda through a toothpaste
    tube onto his brush
        gums left bleeding
Barred by himself
Barred by his gang
Barred by his heroes
Barred by his enemies

Barred by his successors
Barred by his ancestors

He is withheld and held against
    the world
Sitting discreetly in the space between the white and black of
    yin and yang
Curved along the magnetic lines barely touching anything
    almost touching nothing

The plastic spoon in his hand wouldn't dare to dig the
    concrete floor below him
        his fingernails would fall off and rust at the thought of
        scraping his way out

Left with no tools but for his lobotomized brain
    scar tissue indistinguishable from worms
He imagines the undoing of those fatal snips
    reversion to psychosis
Wandering the frantic dimension of ingenious momentum
    working with the mediums of light and speed
Translating it into words
    back to light again

O what a poet would do to see such a schizophrenic scene
    of the greats at their tables floors bars streets
Bottle bag bump bong
    cigarette smoking in 4/5 time to the typewriter
Hallucinations gathered in bleeding palms
    thrown at the wall to see what sticks
Carve the rest into horns and strings
    chisel them into the alphabet rearranged
Eat them like a sunny side up egg at 2 am
    on a Monday morning

O, mother we've missed it I know
    the words have been used
Syntax expired
    language retired

O, father we missed it
        o, sister brother mister I tell you
We missed it
        and we have ourselves to blame
Only ourselves
        and us again

Moments Between Moments

Moments
between
moments
accumulated
like beads of
water holy
left on an
alter what
exists in the
times none see
presenting only an
exoskeleton
autopilot
waiting to
start up again
I suppose the
floating
of leaves
only occurs to
appease
the trees

                                        shedding
                                 knots shaking
                               like weakened
                             knees I suppose
                                 the ground
                                    takes in
                                   footprints
                                 left by in-
                                 between-
                                   ing feet
                                     sinking
                           for simply the
                                 idea of a
                                   moment
                                     passed
               moments between moments
                           alone in thin
                       air incapacitated
                                    holy
                         drops of water
                           evaporated

Head in the Sand

I've been carrying around an aquarium filled with sand
gathered from all the beaches I've combed

I never remember to look at the ocean
I never remember to look in your eyes

I'm too busy with my head bent down
filling my hands
filling my pockets

I used to collect shells and sea glass
but there were never enough

So instead I collect sand
'til my coat is heavy and your hands go cold

And I walk from beach to beach
filling this glass aquarium, watching

The sun move in golden circles
mocking the halo I continue to dodge

And at the end of each day I lay
my head in this sand

Dreaming that yesterday isn't gone
and tomorrow isn't coming

Burning Too Long

I woke up to the smell of electrical fire
    it was my eye sockets
        burning from being plugged in
    too long

I sat down to the smell of fresh asphalt
    it was my hands
        burning from holding my coffee
    too long

I walked the beach to the sound of
    thunder
    it was my heart
        burning from being empty
    too long

I laid down to the touch of dried leaves
    it was my lungs
        burning from smoking
    cigarettes
    too long

I fell asleep to the taste of treated wood
    it was my soul
        burning from being walked on
    too long

I dreamt of electrical fire
    burning
    too long
    so long

Winter Slugs

Slugs of rain are inching down my passenger seat

projected from the flickering street light   above

The rain today acts as though the sun wasn't out yesterday
   the rain today is a horizontal   coloured   grey

    The rain today comes in all directions and sizes
              it is up to me
            to feel attacked
                or held
             To feel warm
                or wet

       The rain today is a blanket
    Dripping down my passenger seat
       Winter   slugs

        The rain today is longer
        than the sun yesterday
          Slugging down
           my windows
        Slugging towards
             spring

        Winter   slugs

Music Goes

I want to go to the place music goes after it is played
    evaporate into a space
    nothing to reverberate off of,
    just a note floating in a realm infinitely
    undefinable from anything else
    identifiable as all
    is and is not
    to be and be not
O, I want to go to the place music goes after it is played
    Yes, I want the song to end

III: LOVE

Liebestraum
On hearing "Liebestraum" by Arthur Rubinstein

I was thinking about imperfections
    writing about mistakes
how I love them
    how I love things to be less than perfect
for their consistency
    the reliability
of fault

I was talking about broken things
    singing off key
how I hear them
    how I hear the staccato better
for its silence
    its moments
of purity

When all of a sudden I was caught
    in *Liebestraum*
love dream
    thinking of you
talking of me
    writing in blood
singing under water
    incredibly imperfect
terribly mistaken
    a love dream
in perfect correlation
    a reliable constellation
Liebestraum
    love dream
mistaken
    I must be

Glass Castle

I play with words in my mouth when you're around
because you listen with red ears
I fumble and spit them out
but you wait until I find the ones that feel right
smooth and soft like skipping stones

In return, your sentences surround me like glass walls
I can see the world through them
but they seclude me
the view from inside steals my breath
and I shiver from the lack of insulation

The scary thing is, I can see myself living in your glass castle
I want you to ask me to stay
because I would
I know the cold would get to my bones, being there alone
but if you offered
I would

I'll keep practicing skipping my stones
while you continue to build this glass castle
just beware, my aim isn't very good
and glass tends to shatter with force

I've Got a Flower in My Palm

I've got a flower in my palm
blooming between my knuckles
petals dripping like blood
keeping me calm
my knees snap when it rains
but I'll happily drown in this flood

I've got a flower in my palm
   digging roots in my worry lines
      photosynthesizing with the light shining through my skin
   trying to keep calm
      so tiny in the shadow of a forest
just a velvet stem dangerously frail and thin

I've got a flower in my palm
wilting beneath callous
I wish to reach out my limp arm
I never could keep calm
I think of presenting you with this corolla in my flesh
but worry you'd look upon it like a cheap charm

I've got a flower in my palm
buried in dirt
I've got a flower in my palm
I've got a flower in my palm
keeping me calm
I've got a flower in my palm
stay calm

I'm In Somebody's Love

We are so consumed by our own loves and obsessions, we don't even consider that we, ourselves, may be the subject of another's dreams.

Grave Digger

His hands are black and rigid
a heart stuck beneath his fingernails
for his incessant grave digging
deaf to her   sorry wails
the body so   nearly decomposed
he was unable   to notice the loam
give way   to flesh
as he searched for   something unknown
At each day's end he   scrubs his hands
picking her dried   blood off in flakes
unaware of   its recent life
unaware of her   dirty mistakes
His hands are red   and dripping now
eyes colourblind and   confused of mud
while her lids   close under worms
where tears   would have flood
The body so   stiff and cold
she takes pleasure   in his touch
softer than   the beetles'
her heart and   his nearly flush
He continues   to dig
beyond her
until she is a pile of dirt behind
and left in her torture

Questions to the Lunar Eclipse

The anticipation of this cosmic wonder
lets slip a raw question
from his drawn mouth

Why do I feel bad when I make people feel bad

He balances his nose between his thumb and forefinger
shelves his eyes on the back wall of his skull

I watch him from the red glow of the eclipse
hiding his thoughts beneath the shadow of his sleeve
eating his cigarette butts and smoking his fingers to the bone
his thoughts are so heavy I hear them hit the ground each
time they roll

Tonight all eyes are on the sky
the moon a rose petal plucked from its stem
but his eyes are reading his palms in the dark
and mine are rendering him into words
so I may carry him in my papers
for when he may go
for if he never arrives

Winter Dream
To...Him
> *(On Reading "Winter Dream", Arthur Rimbaud)*

One day, soon I dream,
we will take a trip
    together
        you and I

We may not go anywhere far,
    maybe visit the ocean down the road
but I will read you poems
    and you will get drunk
    on my words

I'll taste their sweet flavour
    dripping from your lips
and forever we will pass them
    between our bodies, making them one
until language is muddled
    and mouths are lost
    in salty waves

I'll see the shadows lurking in the water
and you'll paint them azure
    together
        we'll swim

Wish I Could Write How I Think

My head is flowing like spring runoff and I want it to soak paper but by the time I've found a pen I thought all the thoughts and God please don't make me think them again I know they'd make good art but they make bad days and what really is art anyways if not bad days turned into something hopefullessnessly nice that probably nobody sees and only loves when you're dead that's fame I guess death doesn't look so bad from this point of view I'm sick of art but without it man everything'd be so grey I hate grey it's like it forgot what it was doing just gave up it's really too bad those thoughts roll in so hot and boiling all day they just never make it to the page in time they cool down with ink and I don't want to think them all over again if I don't have to but shit I do have to if I want to make them worth anything like time at least and here I am at work at 8:30 in the morning getting angry when customers interrupt my writing and thinking but how'd they ever know I was having a bad day I can't stop smiling for the life of me and this one regular I always forget his name well he's probably in love with me and it makes me sad to think that anyone could be in love with me hopelessly the way I am in love with you hopelessly and nothing's ever gonna happen and I guess I'm not the only one feeling this kinda feeling but I wonder how he deals with it I wonder how I deal with it cause I'm still so damn helplessly hopeful that you're hopelessly in love with me too and maybe we both think nothing's ever gonna happen but I guess that means nothing probably ever will but then again maybe that's better than whatever kinda something would happen God dammit these customers just keep walking up and waiting

Your Voice

Your voice carries a melody
that means every note
steady as a breeze carrying a crow,
smooth as the follicles of its feather.

Regardless of language
your voice resounds truth;
it never climbs upon another,
it never cracks from over use.

The way it mixes into your smile,
like stirring cool milk into a steaming cup of tea.

Your voice carries with it
the sound of quiet footprints on fallen leaves;
of ocean foam on sand, left behind by the tide.

Your voice carries an archive
of everything I could ever wish to hear.
Even music has become lost since you spoke,
it has sat down at your feet,
cross-legged like a child,
notepad and pen in hand, begging:

> *Please, sing to me again*
> *the scrupulous song of your voice.*

Things You Fell in Love With (Not Me)

Have you noticed the gifts I have left you
        in the seams
                of your pillows?
The trinkets and clouds gathered in my woven basket
        tucked beneath
                your dreams?
I have gathered every song
        your eyes
                drifted into,
Each sunset that left you crouched
        on a rock
                hit by waves,
                        silently grateful
                              for a fight you knew
                      you'd lose;
All the stars that reflected off
        your chin
                gazing up at them.
Have you noticed me trailing behind you
        picking up all the things
                you fell in love with?
I hold onto them and wait
        to give them back
                after you have forgotten.
I want to see you fall in love
        with them
                again.
I want to see you fall in love
        when I
                am near.

Cinnamon Skin

My skin is rolling
    like the drying bark of a cinnamon tree
    at the colour in your eyes
    and the fragmented words
    between them
                               My knuckles are cracking
                      like wet firewood under December's rain
                                     at the sky's clouds
                   and the way your chin mimics them
                            in an accidental kind of way
My knees are folds
    like the ones left in bedsheets
    at the crack of dusk's eyes
    and the light of Saturn's rings
    sized to the devil's fingers
                                     My feet are white
                                       like frothed milk
                             at the cold beneath them
                       and the six foot deep hole
                                            ahead
O my skin is rolling
    like the drying bark of a cinnamon tree
    your head resting against it
    asleep in summer's clammy palms
    daydreaming of winter's wet arms

Someone is Talking to Me, I am Looking at Them

There was frost on all the windows when I woke up
    it was rain last night

The kettle is boiling already
    a smoke lit between blue fingers

There is frost on the rocks when I go outside
    it was rain last night

The sun hung itself already
    someone is talking to me
    I am looking at them

There are ripples across the harbour when I go into town
    it was still a moment ago

The birds are diving already
    engines bark and dogs groan somewhere

There are ripples across the bay when I'm working
    it was still a moment ago

The fishermen are drenched already
    someone is talking to me
    I am looking at them

The sun has dropped from the gallows
The fishermen are drying their waders
Someone is talking to me, I am looking at them

    their mouth is moving
    like a sailboat in a storm
    eyes dangling like two North stars
    eclipsing the moon
    above malignant waves
    I lay in the bow
    watching above
    they are still talking
    I am still looking

    moon crossing the sky
      stars in tow

There is frost on the constellations
    it was rain last night

There are ripples across the moon
      it was still a moment ago

I'll lay on this sailboat forever
    while they are talking to me
    and I am looking at them

Arborescent Crows

Crinkling like an accordion
Beneath the weight of his fingers
She erupts in silent arias

Opening her marbled eyes
She finds herself upon a menagerie of crows
black as her self
caged in the sky

His fingers become branches
And her body arborescent
And together they build nests
between the iron rods
anchored in the clouds

IV: REMAINS

On Watching the Sunset

I looked at the sun and wished I could go where it was going
I saw the birds and wished I could sit in the sky with them
I saw the wind drawing itself on the flattened waves and
wished I could be light enough for it to carry
I am so tired of this weight
I am so tired of this skin feeling like stone

At these thoughts the sun shone directly on my face and the
wind blew so hard I teetered
my ears burned and popped

It was no use
I stayed with my feet sinking in the sand and the feeling in my
fingertips
I felt as though the ocean was trying to grant my wishes
but the tide wasn't strong enough
and alas
here I am left
to continue

In the Water

I fill my ears incessantly with noise
>to distract the incessant thought

>>ballads and stories
>>whimpers and worries

>>flints and smoke
>>someone spoke

Not me

>>I never speak
>>to myself, that is

>>it is someone else
>>someone farther

It is that someone looking back
>a reflection in the water

Olfactory Hope

I watched the sun rise into the snow clouds
like an egg yolk cracked
on a dream-stained pillow
The mountains wore these clouds as proud hats
as their trees were dyed white for winter
Until they rolled off behind the blue in the sky
headed nowhere
The forest stood higher with his fresh coat
high enough for the whole town to see
from below
The egg began to sizzle and fry on the empty pan behind it
letting the snow drip like melting butter
into the afternoon
And this is how I remembered what hope felt like
the way you remember a smell
in the absence of its scent

Looking So Far Near

We were driving in the dawn
As we always did,
Reflecting ourselves along the lakeside
Until it became the river
And rapids blurred our details.

Your eyes were velvet
Imitating tree tops scattered on mountains
And glaciers filling with fresh winter;

Mine were feathered with the white of an eagle
In the wet glass of the windshield.

Your eyes always did that,
Looked so far away,
Saw things so high up,
So small.

Mine never were so good,
Only seeing what's right in front of me,
Things so close,
So big.

We were driving in the dusk,
You saw the stars as always,
I saw black dust.
Your eyes always did that,
But mine maybe never could.

Life is Round

Rolling Rounds of Rubble Rippling Ruefully Round Reeds

r r r r r r r r r r r r r r r r r r r

Life is round
Life is rolling
Life is round
Life is rubble
Life is round
Life is rippling
Life is round
Life is rueful
Life is round
Life is reeds
Life is round

r r r r r r r r r r r r r r r r r r r

Rolling Rounds of Rubble Rippling Ruefully Round Reeds

A Christmas Carole (Beautiful and Alone)

It is Christmas morning
    Tom Waits is stamping out the smoking butt of his
voice   in my ear drums
    and ash is falling from the sky in crystals too small for
    the
        human eye
The crows are scraping their beaks along the horizon
    shredding the clouds to let in the sun
It sounds like fingernails on a chalkboard
    muffled by the white walls of winter
I squished a mandarin orange on top of my wood stove so my
    hand would smell festive as it fried
The record ended and I am alone again until I flip it and
actively
    beg for more
        the crows did a nice job

O god how can everything be so beautiful
    when I am so alone
It is one thing to claim ignorance to holidays
    to put a burnt palm in Santa's rosy red face
And another thing completely
    to be counting the minutes on a sundial made of snow
    melting Christmas Day away
    crouched and watching with your shadow

It is Christmas afternoon
    Chopin is playing my yellowing teeth like an old grand
        piano
    and the wires are pulling out my eyelashes with each
note
        played
    one by one
    and all together

O why must everything stay so beautiful
    when I am so alone
    killing me with its glow and grace

    the love of it all
    burdening my sorrow
    my black button eyes and stitched seams
    sit wearing away on the shelf
    watching it all go by

O how beautiful it all is
    how beautiful and alone

Looking Asleep

Looking, looking, looking
>always looking for something

In my dreams you visit
>and tell me too look

I wake up
>and ask what for

You never stay
>when I open my eyes

I spend my days
>looking, looking, looking

For you
>to find out what it is

We are looking for
>for you

I go to sleep
>looking, looking, looking

For us
>looking

Wired Skies

Telephone wires make cut-outs of the sky

                organizing the clouds

                              as a golden collage.

I place frames around each section

                painting them crimson and mint

                        to later give away on the

street

                free of charge

     a tip if they please.

The slices of sky fall into postcards and letters

                     or become trapped behind dusty

glass

    while my hat lies empty on the sidewalk

                    and the clouds replace themselves

above.

        Do the telephone wires ever tire

                  of cutting tiny pictures from a

whole?

          Does the sky ever wish

to simply be left alone?

Untitled

I asked a crow to carry me home
and teach me another language
He cawed and guffawed and flew high above
to cradle the sun in his beak
When he returned the ground had crumbled
and my body hovered still
I opened my mouth he opened his beak
and the sun dropped into my throat
Now not only the ground but the sky and the sea
have fallen from all around me
I am left alone in this blank space
with words and birds to carry me

Customer Servitude

hey how's it going
good you
good thanks have a good day
you too thanks hello how are you
good
have a good one
uh-huh thanks
hey how're ya
good and you
good thanks have a good day
thanks you too
okay hello how are you guys today
good yourself
good thank you have a nice day
you as well thank you hi howsit goin
good thanks
bye okay hello how're ya
good good nice day hey no rain yet
yeah real nice no rain ha ha alright well have a good one
yep you too thanks
hello how are you
good good bye
okay bye then oh hey again
hello how are you today
good thanks you
good no rain ha
yep no rain okay well bye
hello how are you doing
good yourself
oh pretty good

Put me in a Box

Put me in a box!
I plead to the masses
Of cow shit in an empty field

Put me in a box and I will play house!
I shout at mothers
Forgetting their children in grocery stores

Put me in a box, dear god, this endless space is too much to fill!
I whimper to the Indian ink
Spreading over pre-drawn outlines

Put me in a box so I may finally feel edges!
I say to the clouds
Closing in on my irises

Put me in a box, you don't even need to wrap it!
I beg Santa Clause
Who is just a fat man working at the mall

Put me in a box and I will call it home!
I say to the holes in my boots
Threatening my toes with frostbite

Put me in a box and store me in your closet!
Put me in a box!
I don't care where
Put me in a box!
Just to leave me there

Dreams//Memories

Dreams are rolling in as if memories
Memories appear like dreams

I no longer know when I am sleeping
I can only hope to be awake

Although none of it seems to matter
For you arrive endlessly

You arrive now
Eyes wide open and closed shut

Sit

Crystals sit in candle holders
    burning eyes
    collecting wax

        Broken teeth sit in ashtrays
            smoking mouths
            piling ash

                Ghosts sit at dinner tables
                    shadowing bodies
                    composting bones

                      Strings sit in guitar cases
                          harmonizing screams
                          tuning steal

                          Books sit in fireplaces
                            typing lies
                            reading truths

                So where then do I sit among these
                                      relics
                                        living
                                  symbolism
                                      dying
                              memorabilia

Lotus

Petals are slipping off this ever floating lotus
Gliding into water with grace
Bloomed from immortal seeds
To feed the roots of its womb
Endlessly living and dying

Living and dying
It floats atop the pond unnoticed
Petals timing their fall around each other
Avoiding velvet collisions
And praying upon misgivings

The lotus floats
The ripples tickle its leaves
And petals sleepily crumple
As new ones bloom in cotton coats
And Van Gogh said
    life is round

What is a Voice Pt. 2

Do you have something to say?
Because I don't have anything to say.

To have a voice is to simply speak.
Words are tools and wisdom
compressed into smudges and smears
meant to be deciphered
and listened to by red ears.

Say something for the sake of it,
don't fret over changed meanings
or mistaken sounds.
Speak to hear your own vibrations,
forget about the fragility of its source.

I don't have anything to say
and I'd like that to be heard
for no reason why,
other than I don't know how to stop
now that I've begun;

because you don't have anything to say either
and here we stay up all night
writing novels with our mouths
'til the clouds look like pages
and the stars illuminate words.

Notes from a Nap on the Beach

Weeping willows are in the sky
        and wind is in the sea

I close my eyes and footsteps become the air
        beneath a birds' wing

I open them and fairies flutter
        over my sun-stroked retinas

The ocean is here to meet me
        and leaves as I met it

It is returning to envelop me now
        in its soft grip

It is saying hello as if it is me
        and I am it

A Poet's End

Studies show the creative mind
        is preserved in a liquid of vulnerability
        of that god awful demon
        whispered as melancholia
        a chalk walled penitentiary
        with a hint of bohemian
        draped in anhedonia
Poets to the latter of prose specifically
        are said to be cursed of this disease
        so often are they in a ponder
        of all things that may mean nothing
        their thoughts like to tease
        and oh they love to wander
        because it simply must mean something
This historical battle of science and romance
        beating each other with dead horses
        and curling up together inside them after
        they never let their love rest
        but they must determine what forces
        have concocted all this matter
        therefore leaving us oh so depressed
Yes I believe it is with ill intention
        such a terrible demise has been given
        to that of a poet so soft
        by the hand of psychology so stiff
        yet I admit it isn't hidden
        what can be such a terrible cost
        of making the unwritable written

Old Friends

Sometimes a dead ghost
is still alive
and resurrects its bones
before your eyes
in the blue of a cemetery night
and the red of a rose's corolla

In this garden of Death's
lie insects in 6-foot-deep canyons;
a galaxy of eyes looking up,
an enchanted smile looking down

Sometimes a dead ghost
is still alive

ABOUT ATMOSPHERE PRESS

Atmosphere Press is an independent, full-service publisher for excellent books in all genres and for all audiences. Learn more about what we do at atmospherepress.com.

We encourage you to check out some of Atmosphere's latest releases, which are available at Amazon.com and via order from your local bookstore:

Until the Kingdom Comes, poetry by Jeanne Lutz
Warcrimes, poetry by GOODW.Y.N
The Freedom of Lavenders, poetry by August Reynolds
Convalesce, poetry by Enne Zale
Poems for the Bee Charmer (And Other Familiar Ghosts), poetry by Jordan Lentz
Serial Love: When Happily Ever After... Isn't, poetry by Kathy Kay
Flowers That Die, poetry by Gideon Halpin
Through The Soul Into Life, poetry by Shoushan B
Embrace The Passion In A Lover's Dream, poetry by Paul Turay
Reflections in the Time of Trumpius Maximus, poetry by Mark Fishbein
Drifters, poetry by Stuart Silverman
As a Patient Thinks about the Desert, poetry by Rick Anthony Furtak
Winter Solstice, poetry by Diana Howard
Blindfolds, Bruises, and Break-Ups, poetry by Jen Schneider
Songs of Snow and Silence, poetry by Jen Emery
INHABITANT, poetry by Charles Crittenden
Godless Grace, poetry by Michael Terence O'Brien
March of the Mindless, poetry by Thomas Walrod
Saints of Sacred Madness, poetry by Joyce Kessel
Thirst of Pisces, poetry by Kate March

ABOUT THE AUTHOR

Amika Caruso is a 23-year-old woman from interior British Columbia. Raised in the mountains, she cherishes the pleasures of solitude and nature for their inspiration. She has been filling journals with romantic language since childhood, writing nearly as many pages as she reads. Caruso is currently studying for her BA in English while living in the small island town of Ucluelet, meaning "people with a safe place to land," on the traditional territory of the Yuułuʔiłʔatḥ.

CPSIA information can be obtained
at www.ICGtesting.com
Printed in the USA
BVHW050217041022
648585BV00009B/21